All Behavior is Communication

How to Give Feedback, Criticism, and Corrections That Improve Behavior

Carmen Y. Reyes

License Notes

This book is intended for professional enrichment. You may not reproduce this book except for teaching purposes. Duplication of this book for commercial purposes is not allowed. Thank you for respecting the hard work of this author.

© 2012 by Carmen Y. Reyes

Copyright © 2010 by Carmen Y. Reyes

SolidRock Press

Contents

Introduction
    5

1. Feedback
    9

Kinds of Feedback
    11

Examples of the Three Kinds of Feedback
    12

More Guidelines for Giving Corrective and Supportive Feedback
    13

2. Criticizing Children
    27

Kinds of Criticism
    28

Guidelines for Criticizing Children
29

3. Correcting and Redirecting Behavior
41

Guidelines for Correcting Behavior
44

Giving Warnings
56

Some Guidelines for Giving Warnings
57

Using Precorrection
58

References
61

About the Author
63

Connect with the Author Online
65

Introduction

Classroom learning is fifty percent content or instruction and fifty percent context or environment. To maximize overall classroom performance, keeping *all* students focused, engaged, and receptive to learning, teachers must be able to walk, smoothly and effortlessly, the very fine line between what teaching methodology is (content) and what emotional atmosphere is (context). In other words, to reach the right balance content-context, teachers need to pay attention equally both to what we are teaching, or the methods we use, and to *how we are teaching it* (how students receive our instruction) or the environment around us. All teachers know very well that, without the right environment, not even the best methodology survives. The fifty percent of learning comprised in our teaching methodology is beyond the scope of this guide, but the fifty percent that is communication-based, most specifically, the *messages we are sending daily to children* takes center stage here. At the core of this language-based approach for improving classroom behavior is the strong belief that teachers' supportive verbal exchanges with students are our most important tool for eliciting the behavior we want from children.

All Behavior is Communication: How to Give Feedback, Criticism, and Corrections that Improve Behavior is a guide about how teachers can use these common ways of talking to help children better themselves. When students show recurrent behavior problems, weak interpersonal skills, and/or seem to lack motivation in improving their behavior it may be beneficial for teachers to reflect about whether the messages sent to children may be a contributing factor in their weak compliance and/or low motivation to improve. Specifically, teachers benefit in analyzing, and if necessary, modifying, the kinds of *behavior expectations* that we are communicating to children, for instance, any low and/or negative expectation that makes our habitually disruptive student aware of our own doubts and skepticism about the child's ability to modify the problem behavior. The way we report to our habitually disruptive students both their current behavior and their chances to improve that behavior; that is, the way we give feedback, criticize, and/or correct the problem behavior are decisive factors in winning children's compliance and in improving motivation. Through corrective feedback and redirection, teachers can send "just the right message" to challenge the child's self-doubts; to change behavior, *children need to believe that success is within their reach.* Most specifically, consistently and enthusiastically we communicate *goal-oriented* (what we want the child to accomplish) and *effort-oriented* (report of progress) messages that we deliver through corrective verbal interventions such as feedback and constructive criticism.

Communication that improves behavior sees behavior change as a *process*, with different children moving at a different pace and rate. Being supportive of children throughout this process is by far more effective than just focusing on the outcome. *All Behavior is Communication:*

How to Give Feedback, Criticism, and Corrections that Improve Behavior breaks down these three common speech acts and presents ways in which teachers can use language that supports and inspires children to be the best they can be.

1
Feedback

When teachers give effective feedback, we are delivering *explicit information* about how appropriate or inappropriate a behavior or an academic skill is. Baker (1999) found that students liked to receive positive feedback, and that students rated their relationship with their teachers higher, when the teacher gave feedback and praised children. Effective feedback, that is, feedback that gives information stated clearly and explicitly, associates with classroom behavior that is both positive and task-appropriate in those students with behavior deficits (Beyda, Zentall, and Ferko,

2002). According to these authors, *information-explicit management*, or giving clear directives to students, decreases task avoidance and off-task behaviors. Both low ability and habitually disruptive students benefit when the teacher consistently uses *reminders* that specify what the students need to be doing. An information-explicit practice such as feedback is of particular benefit to students with behavior difficulties, because it *structures* appropriate behavior at the same time that identifies what inappropriate behavior and/or inadequate performance is.

In addition to being *information-specific*, effective feedback is both *issue-focused* (specifics about performance) and based on *observations*, never focused on the person (child's identity or character) or based on our opinions, judgments, or feelings. Judgments and opinions that are *positive* belong in the category of *praise* (e.g., "You are so organized!"), not feedback. Similarly, judgments and opinions that are *negative* seem closer to *negative criticism* than to feedback (e.g., "You are such a messy-sloppy!"). Either way, praise and negative criticism are general, vague, focused on the child's identity/character, and they state nothing else than our own opinions and feelings. Information-specific feedback, on the other hand, is delivered in a way that students *learn something*, increasing the chances that children will produce an improved response in a similar situation in the future. Most specifically, children need to know what they need to improve and *what exactly they can do* (steps and/or strategies) to improve their current performance. Remember that without any relevant and specific information, you are only giving praise or negative criticism.

Kottler and Kottler (2002) state that teachers should couple feedback with a supportive comment. *Supportive feedback* is sensitive and provides emotional support to the student receiving the feedback; for example, "One of the things that you do that I really like is…"

Kinds of Feedback

The three kinds of feedback that teachers most commonly use in the classroom are:

1. *Positive Feedback* or *Praising*; that is, giving thanks to the student or showing appreciation for an appropriate behavior.
2. *Negative Feedback* or *Criticism.* Negative feedback draws attention to negative behaviors and is

delivered mainly as a reprimand, using a nasty or a sarcastic tone of voice.

3. *Corrective Feedback* or telling the student exactly what to do.

Examples of the Three Kinds of Feedback

I. *Positive or Praise*: I really like the way Sammy raises his hand when he want to share something with this class.

Negative or Criticism: Stop calling out!

Corrective Feedback: I call on students with their hands raised.

II. *Positive or Praise*: Ricky scored a hundred on his spelling sheet. Way to go, Ricky!

Negative or Criticism: Numbers 2 and 5 are misspelled.

Corrective Feedback: Try number 2 and number 5 again. Remember the rule for the "silent e" words.

III. *Positive or Praise*: Alligators and Ninja Warriors just earned another token for good behavior. Good job!

Negative or Criticism: Stop wasting time!

Corrective Feedback: Please get ready. Open your math reference books on page 37.

When we give corrective feedback, *we tell the child exactly what to do*. Corrective feedback is *descriptive*, guiding the student towards a more appropriate alternative or a new behavior. We should deliver corrective feedback in a neutral or positive tone of voice, conveying the expectation that the student will comply with our directives.

More Guidelines for Giving Corrective and Supportive Feedback

Comment about behavior; feedback should give information about the *specific behavior* or the *specific skill* that we expect the child to improve. Statements like, "I like what you did" or "That was nice" are too vague to be good feedback. The child will have a really hard time trying to figure out and to comply with directions that we do not state clearly.

Similarly, messages like, "You need to improve your behavior," "You need to return your homework on time," and "You need to check your spelling" are not corrective feedback. With these kinds of messages, we let the child know that something is not right, but we are not reporting exactly what went wrong, neither how it can be fixed. Giving clarity about what happened should be the aim of our feedback.

With our corrective and supportive feedback, we always remind children what the academic or behavior goal is, meaning that, to give feedback that makes a difference, both the student and the teacher *need to have the child's goal in mind*. Teachers should structure feedback around the child's goal (what the child can do to come closer to the goal), focusing the child on strategies to reach the goal and staying away from what the child did wrong, or what the child must stop doing. Just by reminding the child of what the behavior or academic goal is, we help identify aspects of his behavior that are helpful, as well as identifying and eliminating those behaviors that are not helping.

If all that we do is praising children, eventually, the motivation of our habitually disruptive student or our low-performing student fades away. Just think about it, how we can expect students to *stay focused on effort and goals* if they do not know how close from the target behavior or from the goal they truly are. This does not mean that we should not praise children; praise has a role in motivating children, and there is nothing wrong in enthusiastically praising our students' accomplishments. What it means simply is that we should deliver praise in a way that reinforces our feedback, for example, telling the child, "I love what you did this morning! *Walking away from a fight* showed courage." Instead of just saying, "Good job," tell the child that he used a specific strategy or a specific procedure in a way that gave him success.

Focus the student on *strengths*, making the child aware of how her particular strengths can help in achieving her behavior or academic goal.

Focus your feedback on building and reinforcing strengths rather than on "fixing" weaknesses. To be able to focus on the child's strengths, we need to spend time *finding those strengths*, or finding out *what children can do well* on the specific task, skill, or behavior. Once we identify strengths, the next step will be to analyze how the child can apply those strengths to the part of their behavior or academic performance that needs to improve. And right there, we can create a truly encouraging and inspirational feedback session, working with the child in figuring out ways in which he/she can use those strengths across different areas of school performance.

Describe ways in which the behavior *did match the skill*, including the degree (e.g., good or fair) to which the performance matched the skill or goal. For example, "Today, you were able to remain seated for seven minutes in a row. That's an improvement from four minutes in a row yesterday." For an academic skill, you would say, "Your summary of the story was good because you included..."

Describe ways in which the performance *did not match the skill*; for example, "You need to improve..." or "Your summary was missing..."

Provide a *specific recommendation* for change; that is, a step, a strategy, or a technique that the student receiving the feedback can follow to improve the performance or to approximate the goal. For example, "You seem to focus better when you sit on the reading center. Would you be willing to try that strategy?"

A simple *procedure* to structure the way we give feedback can be, first, make a comment on a positive aspect of the child's performance (the way the performance matched or approximated the skill). Next, give a specific recommendation for change, that is, what the child can do to match the skill more closely. Alternatively, we can: (a) tell the child clearly what we are looking for, (b) praising what he is doing right, (c) telling what is not right, and finally (d) suggesting new ways for accomplishing the goal. We need to make sure that *the next step* for correcting the behavior has been clearly identified.

Two common ways for giving feedback in a structured and positive way are:

1. *Chronological Feedback* or putting our observations (what we see and hear) in the right order or sequence, replaying the events that happened during _____ back to the student.

2. *Sandwich Feedback* or starting and ending our feedback with a positive comment, and then, we "sandwich" the information about what the child needs to improve in-between the two positive comments.

Be careful with the "overloading" of information or with giving the child too many details in one session. This is particularly relevant when we are handling children with low attention spans. To prevent this from happening, before giving feedback, identify no more than three key points that you want to deliver to the student, and *summarize* your key points at the end of the feedback session. Asking the student for a summary is also a good strategy to check what he understands.

When giving feedback always *begin on a positive note* and focus on positive aspects before identifying the area that needs improvement. Before correcting the behavior, let the child know that you like some aspect of her current or her past performance; for example, "Chelsea, you always keep your homework so neat. This past month, I have noticed that your homework has not been looking the same way." We should always include positive information in our feedback, even when the child's performance was not up to the standard or goal. In addition, we should deliver verbal feedback as close in time as possible to the skill or the behavior we are correcting.

Own the feedback by using "I" a lot. Start each key point with an "I-message" such as "I have noticed," "I observed," or "I have seen." "I-statements" help us deliver an assertive (self-confident) message, stay focused on the issue, and get into the specifics. Immediately after the "Iphrase" identify the topic or the issue and follow with a specific of what happened.

With students with recurrent behavior problems, it is extremely important that we give feedback that clearly and explicitly distinguishes between the *intention* of the child's behavior and the *effect* of the behavior. For example, saying, "When you pushed Frankie, you were trying to keep him away from you so that he stopped distracting you from finishing your work (intention of the behavior). It is sad that Frankie bumped his head and now he believes that you wanted to hurt him (effect of the behavior)." In addition, *both you and the child* must be able to separate the child's actions or behavior from his identity or character. For example, saying, "What *you said* sounded mean" (focusing on the action or behavior), not "*You are* mean" (focusing on the child's character).

To keep the child focused on effort, give more feedback about what he is doing right than about what he is doing wrong. With *effort feedback*, we stimulate the correction of errors, helping the child find *alternative solutions* or alternative strategies when the current strategy is not working.

Keep in mind that *feedback on progress* over a number of trials or attempts is more informative and effective than feedback on outcome given in isolation from progress. When we focus children on progress, we are helping them understand the *process*, that is, the actions taken and the procedures implemented to achieve an end, but when we focus children on outcomes (i.e., scores, grades, or comparative norms), we miss the unique opportunity of teaching the value in following steps and in using strategies to achieve the kind of success that, although gradual, is also long-lasting. Feedback that focuses on progress helps children understand that learning new skills or improving their behavior takes time and practice. Teachers' feedback should always aim at helping children discover that *process is more important than outcome*.

Feedback about the processes inherent in the task or skill, also called *cognitive feedback*, help children develop awareness in:

- How they approached the task
- The connection between what they did and the outcome or results; for example, understanding the link between poor effort and a poor outcome

- Possible solutions or alternative strategies

Because constructive feedback is all about processes and procedures, it is never closed and finalized (e.g., "This is it, and this is final"). Quite the opposite, constructive feedback is wide open (receptive) to suggestions and modifications from both the teacher and the student, which means that feedback is constantly evolving.

Ask the child for his opinion and interpretation of the situation. For example, ask, "Tell me, how you feel about what you need to do?"

When we give children feedback about processes and procedures, we should always encourage them to figure out the *reasons for their errors* and/or poor performance. For example, helping the child perceive the relationship between making careless errors in the math test and getting a low score. We should also encourage the child to identify strategies for improvement. Possible learning strategies for improving his performance the next time could be reviewing his answers looking for errors and taking more time to answer the test.

Errors about facts, concepts, or behaviors imply that *doing it differently* (using a different strategy or a different approach) can lead to a better result. Help the child identify what kinds of facts, concepts, or behaviors are particularly difficult for her.

Work in building both *motivational feedback*, or giving feedback that encourages the child either to take action or to stay in course, and *developmental feedback*, or feedback that builds skills. With motivational feedback in particular, we focus the child on his strengths and just by noticing and acknowledging the behavior, we reinforce positive behaviors. Motivational feedback comes first; developmental feedback second.

Aim at encouraging *reflection*. You can use *reflective questions* such as:

1. Did it go as you planned? If not, why not?
2. If you were doing it again, what would you do the same?
3. What would you do differently?
4. How do you feel about trying this strategy/procedure?
5. How do you feel about changing this strategy/procedure?

6. How do you think Frankie feels about the way you reacted/what you said?

7. What makes you think that way?

8. What did you learn from this experience?

Our reflective questions should help children:

1. Engage in the process of change.

2. Understand the procedures they used.

3. Understand the choices they make and the consequences inherent in making particular choices.

4. Identify what they have learned from the experience.

Most importantly, through descriptive feedback that includes reflective questions children should have a clear understanding of *what they are going to do the next time they face a similar situation.*

Teach the child to use *self-reference feedback*. This is one of the most important self-management skills that we can teach to a child with behavior deficits or who is struggling academically, because it helps children see that *they can make progress*. You can model this important skill to the child with statements such as, "I noticed that you checked your answers this time. You circled your final answer, which made your work easier to understand and to grade. Your computation is improving and you made fewer computational errors, which is encouraging. Did you notice how using sample problems on index cards helped you in keeping the right sequence of steps?" Alternative examples are: "Did you notice that you capitalized all your sentences this time? You had trouble with that last time" and "You were able to walk away from trouble when Gregory invited you to a fight. That was hard and you are showing better self-control each day."

Encourage children to use *self-coping statements* similar to the ones above to give themselves feedback both about the quality of their performance (to rate the performance) and about things they can do in a similar situation the next time (strategies and procedures) to improve the performance. I cannot emphasize enough how important self-reference feedback and self-coping statements are, so, if necessary, develop a *feedback checklist* with areas that the child can check to give himself/herself feedback.

Teach children how to ask for feedback; for example, "How does my drawing look?" Alternatively, "Do you want to hear my essay, so you can tell me if I am missing something?"

The literature recommends that teachers keep a ratio of 5:1:0 positive (5) to corrective (1) to negative (0) feedbacks. Some authors recommend that we use a ratio of nine positive comments to each negative or corrective comment we say. Salend and Sylvestre (2005) recommend that we respond to students' incorrect responses by using one or more of three kinds of feedback:

1. *Strategy or Informational Feedback*; for example, "Try another way of doing this."
2. *Effort Feedback*; "You are really working hard."
3. *Ability Feedback*; "You have the skills to do this."

When we use one of these three kinds of feedback, state Salend and Sylvestre, we send the message to our students that failure is the first part of learning, and that errors are a sign that the student needs to work harder.

Always remember that our feedback to a child can take us only a few seconds to deliver, but the effect of that feedback on that child can last *forever*. That is how important all our messages to children are. As a general rule, we should give the kind of supportive and constructive feedback that helps children understand what they need to improve and yet they feel positive about the things they already accomplished.

Feedback, when we deliver it right, is conducive to both improved performance and improved teacher-student relationships.

2
Criticizing Children

We can differentiate between constructive or positive criticism and negative criticism. Constructive or positive criticism is task oriented; that is, focuses the child's attention on the task by pointing out in a specific way what the child did wrong and what he needs to do to fix the mistake. In other words, constructive criticism describes the error and suggests ways for correcting it. Negative criticism, on the other hand, is judgmental in nature, aiming mainly at assigning blame or finding fault in the child. Negative criticism is personality-focused because it references the child's character or how the child is. Negative criticism can be an "attitude" that we show in a variety of ways, including nonverbal messages (e.g., "the look," raising the eyebrow, or the tone of our voice) Constructive and negative criticisms are equivalent to what others in the educational literature call constructive and negative feedbacks.

Kinds of Criticism

The cognitive-behavioral literature distinguishes between four types of criticism:

1. *Permanent*; for example, "What is wrong with you? You *never* listen." (Implying that the attribute or behavior is always the same.)

2. *Changeable*; "Letitia, you are really having trouble concentrating in your class work *this morning*." (Implying that the attribute or behavior can change in the afternoon.)

3. *Global*; "You enjoy messing up for the other kids. You are such a *troublemaker*!" or "You are *smart*, but you are *careless*. Please, follow all the steps."

(Treating the behavior as a quality or a characteristic affecting all areas of performance.)

4. *Specific*; "You are really having a hard time *playing with the other kids*" or "I know you can handle *long division*. You need to slow down so that you do not skip any step." (Implying that the attribute or behavior is local or unique to a particular setting.)

For Seligman, Reivich, Jaycox, and Gillham (1995) the permanent and global types of criticism belong to what they call "pessimistic criticism." This type of criticism references the child's character or whole persona. The authors call the changeable and specific types "optimistic criticism," recommending that teachers and parents deliver only one of these two types of criticism to children.

Guidelines for Criticizing Children

As a rule, teachers and parents should criticize only problems that the child *can solve*. Criticism is a tool to make children aware of what they did poorly.

When criticizing children, use more *observations*; that is, what you see, hear, or can touch, and make fewer evaluations. An evaluation involves making inferences about the things that we observe as well as rating the behavior.

State observations, not interpretations. Observations are what we see happening; interpretations are an analysis or an opinion of what we believe happened. It is important that we state what we notice, not what we think of it. It is also important that we report what we notice at the *concrete* or *sensory level* (can see, can hear, and can touch), not as a representation of the child's attributes or personality (e.g., "*You are* so *mean* to Hector!"). Observations are descriptions of facts; interpretations are fed mainly from inferences, opinions, and judgments.

Use more observation language; that is, concrete information that contributes to the child's learning, and less evaluative language of the kind, good/bad, right/wrong, or correct/incorrect. When we criticize a child, we should be describing the behavior, not judging the behavior.

Pay extra attention to the *manner* in which you are delivering any criticism or feedback to the child. Manner is simply the way in which we say the message. If you did not know yet, you are learning now that *how we say things (the context of the message) often carries more weight than the content of the message, or what we say.* This is a fundamental principle in interpersonal communication- manner is the most important element when we give any kind of criticism or feedback to children.

Make sure that the tone of your voice and nonverbal language carry a helpful attitude.

Have your message clear; which means that, in the first place, *you need to have a message.* The main goal of criticism is to get your message across (what you are trying to convey). If there is no message, then you are just venting anger and frustration. When we criticize a student, we need to have something that we are trying to teach. In one sentence, *if we feel ready to criticize, then we must be ready to teach.*

Never criticize a child if you are not ready to offer ideas, suggestions, alternatives, and/or recommendations for change.

To improve skills in criticizing children, before saying anything to the child, honestly answer: Am I doing this because I feel impatient and irritated, or am I doing this because I have a message to deliver and this is a good time to deliver it? A second self-question to answer is: What do I want to accomplish with my criticism?

When handling acting-out behavior, disruptive behavior, and/or conflict between students, collect the facts *before* you begin criticizing or giving feedback. Take a moment to assess the situation before saying anything to the child or children.

Show concern for the inappropriate behavior rather than showing anger; for example, "I am really concerned about _____." A tone of concern communicates to the child both that he/she is important to us and that we care. On the other hand, a negative tone such as anger, frustration, or sarcasm buries the real message beneath all the noise and harshness.

Always keep in mind that the purpose for criticizing a child is to *develop awareness* that leads to correcting or at least improving the behavior or skill. Simply put, the purpose of criticism is *to correct future behavior*. We need to deliver our criticism and feedback in a manner that shows our concern at the same time that encourages the child to better himself. If we are not doing that, then, we are defeating our own purpose.

When we criticize a student, we need to make sure that we are criticizing the child's *actions* or behavior, not the child's character or who the child is. With both praise and criticism, we should always reference actions, not abilities. Examples of criticism that is character-oriented are:

- You better start acting like a ten years old.
- You have a potty mouth.
- You show no respect for anyone!
- You always have an excuse for not doing your homework.
- You could learn if you pay attention.

Criticizing the child's character sends the message to the student that the deficit in the skill or behavior is permanent and/or global, and *it is not going to change.* This is the exact opposite of the kind of messages that we need to deliver to our habitually disruptive and low-achieving students. With these children in particular, we need to make it clear that we see errors and negative outcomes as *events happening at a particular position in place at a particular time*, not as part of the child's identity.

Messages that criticize character are "you" messages; for example, "*You* have a potty mouth!" or "*You* are always messing up." When there is a strong feeling, it is better if we deliver the feeling using an "I" message instead. An "I" message describes what we are feeling and the reason for the feeling. For example, rather than saying "Don't you dare using that language with me!" say, "I am upset because I do not like being cursed." "I" messages always start with "I feel ____," "I like ____," or "I do not like ____."

When we are handling a strong feeling, it is important to identify the unacceptable behavior (e.g., "That language is inappropriate"), stating our feelings about the behavior ("I feel like leaving the room when I hear that language"), and pointing out an acceptable alternative ("When you talk to me without cursing, I will listen to what you have to say.")

Avoid *generalizations* such as "always" or "never." For example, saying, "You always mess up" or "You never play fair." A more constructive message would be telling the child that when he did X (e.g., waited for his turn to play) the outcome was better (e.g., he enjoyed the game and was able to finish it) than the times when he did not wait for his turn and as a consequence felt disappointed with the results.

Express disapproval for the inappropriate behavior by stating the effect of the behavior on you and/or others; then point out your feelings about the behavior. For example, "Nicky, when you call names, you embarrass other children in the classroom, and I feel annoyed."

Do not engage in name-calling (e.g., "What a potty mouth you are!") or in threats (e.g., "You are really going to get it if you keep that up!").

Minimize the child's errors and mistakes. Use *effort feedback*, and help the child focus on effort or trying rather than outcomes (success or failure). Remind the child that "Tomorrow is another day to try."

When you criticize a child, be specific about the task criticized, and reserve your criticism to those occasions when you feel the child did not show her best effort. Criticism should consist on specific explanations like, "You did not spend enough time in studying for your math test." Praise, on the other hand, can be more global, for example, "You care for your school work and can work hard (Praise). That's why *I expect* from you to spend adequate time studying for tests." In the last sentence, the teacher is reinforcing the message with a *positive expectation*.

Tolerate, rather than criticize, children's negative behaviors. Therapeutic teachers and parents provide a warm, understanding atmosphere that communicates a basic acceptance of children as valuable individuals, even when we disapprove of the behavior.

Remember that we are not going to motivate the child to improve the behavior by making the child feel worse about himself and his behavior.

Keep in mind that, what we focus on, we automatically reinforce, but what we ignore eventually fades away. Our focus should always remain in what children are doing well and in their strengths, rather than what they are doing wrong or their weaknesses. When we concentrate on criticizing negative or inappropriate behaviors, we may inadvertently reinforce those behaviors. On the other hand, simply noticing and praising positive behavior not only increases those behaviors, but also improves our interactions with children.

Always criticize the child in private, not in front of peers.

When criticizing a behavior or an academic skill, identify: (a) the behavior or skill that you *expect* from the child and (b) times when the child displayed the desired behavior. Give at least two positive or supportive *examples* of the target behavior or skill. For example, you would say, "Yesterday, when Gregory challenged you to a fight, you *remained calm* and *walked away*. Those are the kinds of behaviors that show good self-control." In addition, give at least one non-example of the target behavior (what the target behavior is not). Illustrate the behavior that you are criticizing.

Children need to understand what criticism means, and what criticism does not mean. Explain to children that criticism is just one person's opinion about us at a particular time. Criticism is not an accusation of our character, and does not mean that we are totally or permanently the way the other person says we are. Children need to understand that criticism can be a helpful evaluation of how they are doing, and that they can use it to improve their behavior or academic skills.

Teach *relative reasoning*, making sure that children understand that we are all good at doing some things and not so good at doing others. We can do the same thing well sometimes, but not so well at other times.

Become a *coach*; that is, give instructions, facilitate the practice of the skill or new behavior, and finally, give feedback of the child's performance.

Train children in *self-criticism*, so that they discover by themselves what they did wrong. For example, rather than telling a student which math problems are incorrect, you can say, "Find the two problems that are incorrect," or "Find the errors in problems four and seven."

To develop skills in self-criticism, make the habit of asking the child what was the best thing she did and what was her weakest moment.

Link each criticism with a compliment or with praise. In addition, *create a partnership* between criticism and encouragement, and make them walk side-by-side. On the other hand, avoid using criticism and rewards together. To create a criticism-encouragement partnership, some pointers are:

1. Speak the language of effort and always recognize the child's effort.

2. Emphasize the child's progress, letting her know that she is moving in the right direction.
3. Consistently use developmental words such as "growth" and "improvement."
4. Emphasize what the child is doing right.
5. Reassure the child that you are by her side.

Maximize the positive effect of praise. For example, you can praise the child's unique approach to handle a social problem, careful planning, persistence, effort, and/or positive attitude. These are things that the child *can control and can change* when the results are disappointing. Avoid praising ability and "smartness;" there is very little that the child can do to improve innate abilities. Simply put, praise is more effective in influencing positive behavior when it is given to the child within the context of "effort well done." Failure and disappointing results are easier to swallow when it is presented as "effort that needs improvement."

Do *daily reviews*. Each afternoon, or if you are a parent, before bedtime, spend a few minutes talking about the things children did well during the day. Celebrate the positive things without commenting about what went wrong.

3
Correcting and Redirecting Behavior

Behavior and feelings can be seen as two sides of the same coin; the way we behave reflects the way we feel and the way we feel affects how we behave. For instance, if I feel happy, I act cheerfully, but when I am feeling down, my behavior tones down. Adults act this way, and, in coping with feelings and emotions, children are not that different from us. Most adults have words to express all kinds of feelings, but when children do not have the words they need to express how they feel, all that is left out for them are *actions* or behavior, in particular, acting-out behavior. If we are listening empathetically to what children are trying to communicate through their acting-out behaviors, we can pick up the subtle cues that signal when the child feels upset or fearful, and that something simply "does not feel right" to the child. As the title of this book suggests, *there is always a message behind our behavior* and skillful behavior managers understand this and work in finding the message or true meaning implicitly stated in children's behaviors. When teachers understand what students are communicating through the disruptive behavior, we can respond more effectively to the behavior.

Finding true meaning in what the child's behavior communicates (what the child is telling us) is only one aspect of the equation in therapeutic communication; developing awareness about the effect (meaning) of *our own behavior* in the child (what we are communicating to the child through the things we do and the words we say) is equally important. For instance, when the child hears our feedback and criticism, does he hear concern or annoyance; acceptance or rejection? What about the behavior expectations that we are communicating? Are we making the child aware that we believe in his ability to overcome the problem behavior, or are we showing discouragement and hopelessness in his improvement? Expanding the original title of this guide, we can say now that *all behavior is a two-way communication* (from student-to-teacher and from teacher-to-student), and, if we are not careful, our body language, interactions, and verbal exchanges with students may reinforce the very same disruptive behaviors that we are trying to eliminate in the first place. Children learn a lot about themselves (about who they are and why they do the things they do) by listening to the messages that adults in their environment send to them, so, to deliver messages that influence positive behavior, teachers and parents need to articulate those messages in ways that are both optimistic and growth-promoting. This is one of the most fundamental principles in interpersonal communication, and no one puts it better than the neuro-linguistic tradition: *the behaviors we get from children are mainly a reflection of the kinds of messages we send to them* (See for example Mahony, 2003). Negative messages and low expectations elicit negative behaviors; positive messages and high expectations elicit positive behaviors. Therefore, if we are not satisfied with the responses (behaviors) we are getting from our students, our first step in correcting and redirecting that behavior would be for us to *change the kinds of messages we are sending to them.*

Guidelines for Correcting Behavior

Disapprove *the behavior*, not the child. Make sure that the child understands that you feel disappointed with a particular action or a specific behavior, not with the child's whole character or his identity. Provide warmth and an accepting atmosphere that communicate your basic acceptance of the child as an individual even when you disapprove of the child's behavior.

Avoid "you" messages that label the child's character; delete from your repertoire messages such as:

- What a messy sloppy you are!
- You are *always* messing up!
- Can't you do *anything* right?
- You seem to enjoy fooling around and acting silly with your friends.
- You *never* listen to anyone!

- You *always* have an excuse for not bringing your homework.
- You have no respect for *anyone*.
- You are such a liar!

In addition to labeling character, these kinds of messages include words like "always," "anything," and "anyone," implying that the child's behavior is not only permanent but also an inherent trait (like having brown eyes) beyond the child's control.

Replace messages that label character with messages that *label the action* or the child's behavior. For example:

- You are *acting* in a selfish way.
- What you *said* to Devon sounded mean.
- Not wearing a helmet while riding your bike is risky *behavior*.

Keep in mind that the behavior upsets *you*, not the child, so, be careful in not labeling the behavior when you are feeling angry and/or using harsh words. To express your disappointment, use statements such as "I don't like when you curse" or "I feel disappointed when you say lies."

Put emotional distance between the child and the disruptive behavior, making the child aware that although he *does* the behavior, he *is not* the behavior.

One of the most effective ways of separating a child from his disruptive behavior is by consistently talking about the misbehavior using the language of "errors" and "mistakes." Let children know that mistakes are normal; we all make mistakes. Mistakes give us the opportunity to learn and to grow, and from this perspective, we can embrace our mistakes and feel challenged by them, not frustrated, much less intimidated. We know that we have learned something from our mistake when we become aware of *when* to fix it and *how* to fix it.

Give the child the opportunity to fix the mistake. You should have suggestions and alternatives that allow the child to make a right from a wrong. Help the child identify and access positive alternatives.

Show your concern and be constructive; for example, "I am concerned about your behavior."

Empathize and acknowledge the child's feelings; for example, "You look angry, but I cannot let you hit Devon."

Use eye contact, say the child's name, and use pleasant words. Make sure that the tone of your voice carries a helpful attitude.

Stay cool, do not display emotion, and remain calm and business-like.

Do not dwell on the past; correct and redirect behavior that is happening *here* and *now*.

Stay close to the child (at a desk's length), and avoid giving reprimands across the room. Always correct the child in private.

Avoid vague or global statements like "This is sloppily written" or "Be nice to Devon." The child needs to know precisely what he is doing poorly so that he can fix it.

Begin on a positive note. Before correcting the child, let her know that you like some aspect of her behavior, current or past, or let her know of something that she is doing right; for example, "Wow, you worked hard to wipe your desk clean. All that you need to do now is to remove these small spots here." Alternatively, "You need help in handling the subtraction step in long division. All the other steps are fine."

Avoid using negative directions that tell the student what not to do; for example, "Don't make noises" or "Don't hit other children."

Describe what you want the child to do in positive terms. Use *positive wording* that tells the child what he should do rather than what not to do. For example, "Raise your hand to talk" rather than "Don't call out the answers!" With little effort, we can learn to replace a negative direction like "Don't run!" with a positive message such as "Walk."

Use positive direction by guiding the child towards a more appropriate behavior. Give the child the *alternative behavior*; for example, rather than saying, "Don't color on the table," say, "You can color on this paper, not on the table." Alternatively, you can say, "I understand that you feel angry. I cannot let you hit another child, but you can go to the back of the room and kick this toy."

Give the child a simple *choice*. For example, "You can sit *quietly* at the circle or you return *quietly* to your desk and start reading your book." Notice that, regardless of what the child chooses, she still complies with the behavior that we want (being quiet).

Redirect an angry or acting-out child either with a substitute behavior, a substitute toy, or by sending the child to a different area of the room that it is going to help him "feel better."

Use direct statements (e.g., "Keep your voice low") rather than questions ("Would you please keep your voice low?") A question implies that you are giving the child a choice.

Avoid using "why" questions; for example, "Why did you do that?" This kind of questioning only leads to an excuse of the misbehavior.

To express your disapproval for a behavior, make a statement that clarifies to the child the effect of the behavior on you, or your feelings about the behavior. Then, follow with an acceptable alternative; for example, "Nicky, when you leave your seat without permission, I get distracted. *When you return to your seat* and raise your hand, I will listen to what you have to say." Notice that this statement also includes the *expectation* that the child is going to return to her seat.

Give the child *examples* of behaviors you would like her to work on. Give specific examples of what you mean by _____ (e.g., behaving in line or sitting straight).

Additionally, give an example of what you will do to help the child, and examples of what the child can do to improve the behavior. Simply put, the more examples and illustrations you give, the better the chances of improving compliance.

Discuss the problem behavior with the child. We cannot learn from mistakes and negative outcomes if we do not talk about them and analyze them. Only deeper analysis gives important insight and makes apparent what needs to be fixed. Aim at helping children analyze and learn from both their successes and their failures.

Focus children on how they can fix problems. To accomplish this, we need to focus children on *solutions*. For instance, when Lucy spilled her juice, Ms. Anderson labeled the child's character, commenting, "How can you be so careless?" Two days later, when Lucy spilled her glitter, Ms. Wilson delivered a very different message, this time, guiding the child to the solution: "The broom and the dustpan are in the closet." Which of these two messages do you think was more effective in stimulating Lucy's learning? More examples:

- *Ineffective:* Stop pushing other children!
- *Effective:* Please, walk next to me.
- *Ineffective:* Do not dare make another mess!
- *Effective:* Next time, remember to pick up your math manipulatives.

Focus children in how to prevent the same problem from happening in the future. You can select one smaller and doable *next step* for the child to do in a similar situation the next time. For example: "When you tried to stop Frankie from distracting you, he did not understand what you were trying to tell him. You can try saying his name first, so that you are sure you have his attention."

Asking the child for his own solution gets more involvement from the child. Simply ask, "What do you think you can do here?" Then, make sure that you listen to what the child is suggesting and that you incorporate those suggestions in the solution.

When correcting behavior, *make it all about problem solving*. Couple your correction with a systematic approach for solving the problem. You can follow these steps:

- ❖ *Step 1: Acknowledge the Problem.* For example, saying, "I can see that there is a problem. You want to read the book and Gregory has it." Alternatively, "It is frustrating when the blocks don't balance and they keep falling."

- ❖ *Step 2: Ask questions that redirect the child to a strategy, a solution, and/or an alternative behavior.* For example, "Have you asked Gregory to give you the book when he is finished?" Alternatively, "What would happen if you reinforce the column putting extra blocks on the bottom?"

- ❖ *Step 3:* If necessary, *give a solution or show the solution* to the child. For example, "Tell Gregory that you would like the book when he is done reading." Alternatively, "Put these two blocks on the bottom, like this."

- ❖ *Step 4: Summarize,* or have the child *rephrase* (state in his own words) what happened. Say, "Next time, remember what you did here to solve this problem. You felt frustrated because you thought you could not do it, but now you see that you can."

Always remember that the way we respond to students plays a crucial role in the way children respond to us and to each other. When we teach social skills and provide resources that help children overcome obstacles, we are building coping resources that last a lifetime. Analyze what new skills the child should learn to replace the old behavior. In addition, identify ways in which the child can learn the new skill. If necessary, train the student in how to solve social problems. On my free blog, *The Psycho-Educational Teacher*, you will find plenty of insight and the steps needed to teach students the important skill of solving social problems. Once children understand the process inherent in solving social problems it is easier to ask them for suggestions and alternatives to correct their own behavior.

Remind the child of those times when things worked out well. For example, say, "Yesterday, you remembered your homework. What did you do then that you are not doing now?" Help the child recognize which efforts and strategies are effective, so that she does more of what is helping and less of what is not working.

Remind the student of your positive (but realistic) expectation and let the child correct her own behavior. For example, "I trust your ability to clarify this misunderstanding with Camille. I know that you will find a way to do it." Be clear about your expectation (avoiding general and ambiguous language such as "Be nice to Camille"). Focus the child on *one aspect* of the problem or behavior to solve first, not on an area that is so broad that the child is not going to be able to handle it.

Make suggestions such as: "Have you thought of approaching Camille this way…?"

Encourage the child to *evaluate* her performance in coping with the problem. Ask questions such as: Are you satisfied with what you did? Do you feel happy about the result? In addition, ask; is there anything that you would do differently?

When the kid is struggling, do not try to make it less painful by saying that it is going to be easy. Chances are that it is going to remain difficult; you know it and the kid knows it. Acknowledge and validate the way the child is feeling and say, "I understand that this feels hard, but you have shown improvement and I have confidence that you are going to be able to figure this out."

In 1994, Schaefer developed a *six-step approach* to give corrections and reprimands that, with minimal variations, is still relevant:

- ❖ *Step 1*: Point out the behavior that must change.

- ❖ *Step 2*: Explain the reason; for example, "Throwing food in the lunchroom makes a mess" or "Food is for eating, not for playing with."

- ❖ *Step 3*: Tell the penalty; for example, "If you continue throwing food, you will stay in the lunchroom instead of playing outside."

- ❖ *Step 4*: Point out an acceptable alternative; for example, "You can play with cards."

- ❖ *Step 5*: Ask for feedback of how well the child understood; "Now, what did I just tell you?"

- ❖ *Step 6*: Quickly reestablish your bond with the child. You can smile and continue interacting with the child as if anything had happened. About this step, we need to make sure that we maintain a positive relationship with the student. Children respond better to correction and negative consequences when they have a positive relationship with the adult.

We can add two more steps:

- ❖ *Step 7:* If the child does not comply, repeat the initial command, beginning with "You need to…"
- ❖ *Step 8:* After administering the consequence, ask the child what he can learn from the mistake.

Giving Warnings

Avoid giving threats; for example, "You will see what is going to happen if you keep acting that way." Give a warning instead. A warning is a *realistic* statement of an imminent penalty; that is, with a warning, we briefly inform the child of an unpleasant consequence. Effective correction includes a warning about an unpleasant consequence; for example, "If you keep making noises, you will have to go to the time out area for five minutes." Warnings include two parts:

- ➢ *Part One:* A statement of the misbehavior.
- ➢ *Part Two:* The consequence that will be administered. For example:

- I asked you to stop making noises. If you do it once more, you have to go to the time out area for five minutes.

- This is a warning. If you say that word again, you will lose five minutes of your free time.

- You have five seconds to stop _____. If you do not stop by then, you will _____. One… two… three…

Notice that an effective warning has an "if… then…" format. When we use a warning, we are telling the student what will happen if he does not comply. Bloomquist (1996) recommends that we follow this procedure:

❖ *Step 1*: Give a command (a ten words statement of what the child needs to do).

❖ *Step 2*: Follow the command with a warning.

❖ *Step 3:* Follow with a consequence.

❖ *Step 4*: Restate your original command.

Some Guidelines for Giving Warnings

Use only one warning and state the warning only once, or use the *three warnings, then penalty technique*.

Do not reissue, coerce, or give a different warning.

Count aloud to five before administering the consequence.

Deliver the warning in as a calm and positive manner as possible.

Include in the warning a clear statement about what the child must stop doing, and what will happen if the disruptive behavior continues.

Use natural and *logical* consequences. For example, "When you forget to return your book to the shelf, it is difficult to find it the next time you need it."

Do not argue with the child.

After the penalty, ask the child what she learned from the mistake. Avoid asking, "Why did you do that?"

Using Precorrection

Lampy, Fenty, and Beaune (2005) recommend using precorrection. Precorrection is a proactive approach for managing behavior; that is, it is associated with what happens directly before the expected behavior. Correction, on the other hand, is reactive, because it associates with what happens directly after the inappropriate behavior. For instance, when we use precorrection, we remind a student or the class of the appropriate behaviors that we expect before _____ (e.g., lunchtime) or at the beginning of

_____ (e.g., sustained silent reading). In other words, precorrection is *using reminders and prompts* before setting students to complete a task. According to the authors, using precorrection prevents the occurrence of inappropriate behaviors, and sets up situations in which the teacher can use praise to reinforce the appropriate behaviors. From Colvin, Sugai, and Patching (1993) we get the following steps for giving precorrection:

❖ *Step 1:* Identify the context; that is, when and where the predictable or inappropriate behavior happens.

❖ *Step 2:* Specify an appropriate behavior or an alternative that the student or class should use in place of the inappropriate behavior. When choosing an alternative behavior, this new behavior:

2A. Must be *observable*; that is, we must be able to watch what the child does.

2B. Must be *incompatible* with, or the opposite of, the current behavior.

2C. Must fulfill the *same purpose* as the old behavior.

❖ *Step 3:* Change the environment or classroom routines in which the inappropriate behavior happens.

- ❖ ***Step 4:*** Have the child or class practice the new behavior.

- ❖ ***Step 5:*** Provide prompts for appropriate behaviors; for example, "Remember to raise your hand" or "When we get in line, remember to keep your hands to yourself."

5A. If the student or class fails in exhibiting the new behavior, use a reminder; for example, "What do we do if we want to answer a question (or to talk) in this class?"

- ❖ ***Step 6:*** Reward the student or class when you see them exhibiting the appropriate behavior.

- ❖ ***Step 7:*** Monitor progress using charts and stickers.

References

Baker, J. A. (1999). Teacher-student interaction in urban at-risk classrooms: Differential behavior, relationship quality, and student satisfaction with school. *Elementary School Journal*, 100(1), pp. 57-70.

Beyda, S. D., Zentall, S. S., & Ferko, D. J. K. (2002). The relationship between teacher practices and the task-appropriate and social behavior of students with behavioral disorders. *Behavioral Disorders*, 27(3), pp. 236-255.

Bloomquist, M. L. (1996). *Skills training for children with behavior disorders: A parent and therapist guidebook.* NY: Guilford Press.

Colvin, G., Sugai, G., & Patching, B. (1993). Precorrection: An instructional approach for managing predictable problem behaviors. *Intervention in School and Clinic*, 28, pp. 143-150.

Kottler, J. A., & Kottler, E. (2000). *Counseling skills for teachers*. Thousand Oaks, CA: Corwin Press.

Lampi, A. R., Fenty, N. S., & Beaunae, C. (2005). Making the three ps easier: Praise, proximity, and precorrection. *Beyond Behavior*, 15(1), pp. 8-12.

Mahony, T. (2003). *Words work! How to change your language to improve behaviour in your classroom*. Carmarthen, Wales: Crown House.

Salend, S. J., & Sylvestre, S. (2005). Understanding and addressing oppositional and defiant classroom behaviors. *Teaching Exceptional Children*, 37(6), pp. 32-39.

Schaefer, C. E. (1994). *How to influence children: A handbook of practical child guidance skills* (Second Edition). Northvale, NJ: Jason Aronson.

Seligman, M. E., Reivich, K., Jaycox, L., & Gillham, J. (1995). *The optimistic child*. NY: Houghton Mifflin.

About the Author

Carmen Y. Reyes, *The Psycho-Educational Teacher*, has more than twenty years of experience as a self-contained special education teacher, resource room teacher, and educational diagnostician. Carmen has taught at all grade levels, from kindergarten to post secondary. Carmen is an expert in the application of behavior management strategies, and in teaching students with learning or behavior problems. Her classroom background, in New York City and her native Puerto Rico, includes ten years teaching emotionally disturbed/behaviorally disordered children and four years teaching students with a learning disability or low cognitive functioning. Carmen has a bachelor's degree in psychology (University of Puerto Rico) and a master's degree in special education with a specialization in emotional disorders (Long Island University, Brooklyn: New York). She also has extensive graduate training in psychology (30+ credits). Carmen is the author of 60+ books and articles in child guidance, and in alternative teaching techniques for struggling learners. To preview her books, read the complete collection of articles, download *free* skill-building guides, and download *free* lesson plans, visit Carmen's blog, *The Psycho-Educational Teacher*.

Connect with the Author Online

Blog

http://thepsychoeducationalteacher.blogspot.com/

Twitter

http://twitter.com/psychoeducation

Email

thepsychoeducationalteacher@gmail.com

Made in the USA
Middletown, DE
04 November 2021